CHESHIRE'S LAST DAYS OF STEAM
TOM HEAVYSIDE

Birkenhead shed, 18 February 1966. Studying this view of a section of the shed yard at this large motive power depot on what was a drab winter's day, it is hard to believe that within two years steam locomotives had vanished altogether from the Wirral peninsula. Visible are fourteen locos with either a 2-8-0 or 2-10-0 wheel arrangement, while another twenty-five engines were resting out of sight of the camera, many under cover on one of the shed's sixteen roads.

Text and photographs
© Tom Heavyside, 2018

First published in the United Kingdom, 2018,
by Stenlake Publishing Ltd.
54-58 Mill Square,
Catrine, KA5 6RD
01290 551122
www.stenlake.co.uk

ISBN 978-1-84033-802-7

The publishers regret that they cannot
supply copies of any pictures featured
in this book.

Printed by
Berforts, 17 Burgess Road,
Hastings, TN35 4NR

Acknowledgements

I would like to express my sincere thanks to Keith
Gunner along with the staff at Search Engine, National
Railway Museum, York, for their ready help in the
completion of this volume. My very belated thanks are
due to British Railways London Midland Region for the
issue of permits to visit the motive power depots in the
1960s, and to the shed foremen who on other occasions
readily allowed access to their domains when I arrived
on spec!

The Wirral was one of the last stamping grounds for the once 245-strong LMS Hughes/Fowler 'Crab' 2-6-0s. The two that survived into January 1967, Nos. 42727 and 42942, were both attached to Birkenhead shed. Here No. 42942, built at Crewe in 1932, heads back to base tender-first through Hooton station on 22 August 1966.

Introduction

The county of Chester, prior to the redrawing of boundaries in 1974, encompassed an area of land mainly to the south of the River Mersey. In the west the county also included the Wirral peninsula, while in the east a narrow strip of land reached into the Pennines as far as the western end of Woodhead Tunnel. The term 'Cheshire Plains' is an apt description for much of the county.

The first railway laid across Cheshire was that from south of Crewe towards Warrington, opened by the Grand Junction Railway in July 1837. It was later to become part of the important West Coast main line linking London and Glasgow. The subsequent history of the railway companies that eventually had an interest in serving Cheshire is complex, some of them also focusing their sights on the lucrative markets to be had in the growing cities of Liverpool and Manchester on the northern side of the Mersey in Lancashire, as well as the Irish trade via Holyhead. Mention should be made of the Cheshire Lines Committee, a conglomerate formed by the Great Northern, Manchester, Sheffield & Lincolnshire (Great Central from 1897) and Midland railways, which operated the route between Stockport and Chester via Northwich prior to Nationalisation.

A legacy from the early days of the railway era in Cheshire, and the various companies coming under different ownership at the Grouping in 1923, was that the locomotive stock inherited by British Railways at Nationalisation in January 1948 had a somewhat cosmopolitan flavour. For instance in September 1950 the eleven motive power depots spread across the county, all except one then administered by the London Midland Region, were responsible for a total of 491 steam locomotives, of which 345 had an affiliation with the former London Midland & Scottish Railway, ninety-five with the Great Western Railway and forty-six with the London & North Eastern Railway. Five ex-WD 2-8-0s accounted for the remainder. In addition engines from a wide area could regularly be seen either visiting or passing through the county.

Regarding the ex-GWR contingent resident in the county in 1950, fifty-four were based at Chester West, the only shed in Cheshire to come under the jurisdiction of the Western Region, among them three 'Saint', three 'Castle' and eight 'Hall' 4-6-0s. The other forty-one were domiciled at the former joint GWR/LMS shed at Birkenhead, the most notable at the latter being six 'Grange' class 4-6-0s. The engines with a LNER lineage were allocated to Northwich (twenty-nine) and Chester Northgate (nine), both ex-Cheshire Lines Committee depots, with the remaining eight attached to the small former Great Central Railway shed at Bidston. The most prestigious engines with an affinity to the LNER were three 'Director' class 4-4-0s at Northwich.

Towards the end of the decade in March 1959 the same eleven sheds, with Chester West also now under London Midland Region control following its transfer from the Western in February 1958, had a slightly increased total allocation of 503 steam locomotives. While former LMS classes had increased in number to 408, only seventeen bequeathed by the GWR remained, fifteen at Chester West and two at Birkenhead. Inroads into the ex-LNER contingent was equally savage with just two left at Northwich and six at Bidston. Chester West and Birkenhead were still home to some ex-WD 2-8-0s, two at the former and four at the latter, while among the incomers were sixty-four of the BR Standard classes introduced from 1951.

Into the 1960s more and more reliance was made on diesel power, while electric traction was introduced on the lines north from Crewe to Manchester and Liverpool. As a result of this onslaught on steam the doors at Chester West and Chester Northgate sheds were closed to the iron horse in 1960, followed by Macclesfield in 1961, Alsager in 1962 and Bidston in 1963. By May 1965 the surviving six steam sheds in the county were looking after a reduced steam stock of 250, comprising 179 locomotives with a LMS antecedent (some built by BR to the same drawings), along with seventy-one constructed to BR Standard designs. Later that year Crewe North shed said goodbye to steam with activity in the town then concentrated on the South shed.

At the start of 1967 the remaining five sheds still in business had a total of 196 steam locomotives on their books, 131 with a LMS pedigree and sixty-five BR Standards, the latter consisting of four 'Britannia' Pacifics at Stockport Edgeley, two Class 4 2-6-0s at Chester and no less than fifty-nine of the powerful 9F 2-10-0s at Birkenhead. Thus, it was hard to comprehend that the total annihilation of steam was literally only months away, with the iron horse still regularly to be seen hard at work on the

As the 1960s progressed steam power was increasingly sidelined by an ever-growing stock of diesel locomotives and multiple-units, as could be seen at Chester General on 22 August 1966. Seen here standing on the goods line alongside the station, is Stanier 8F 2-8-0 No. 48090 with a train of oil tanks, while of much more recent vintage a diesel multiple-unit awaits custom at platform 13. No. 48090 was often to be seen in the Chester area following its transfer to Mold Junction shed (code 6B), just outside the Cheshire boundary in Wales, in January 1963. When that shed closed in April 1966 it was moved the short distance to Chester shed (6A), before being withdrawn from Bolton (9K) in April 1968.

Wirral peninsula, along the Chester to Stockport via Northwich corridor, and towards Warrington from both Chester and Crewe. But Chester shed closed to steam on 5 June, followed by both Birkenhead and Crewe South on 6 November. Shed closures elsewhere in the surrounding area also had an impact towards the elimination of steam.

By the beginning of 1968 the steam population had declined to just thirty-nine, seventeen Stanier 8F 2-8-0s at Northwich, with another ten 8Fs together with a dozen Stanier Class 5 4-6-0s at Stockport Edgeley. The next shed to sever its association with steam was Northwich on 5 March 1968, Stockport Edgeley soldiering on until its last rites were held on 6 May. However, this was not quite the finale for steam in Cheshire as for a few more weeks Newton Heath shed in Manchester remained responsible for

one or two diagrams that penetrated the north of the county. In fact on Sunday 4 August 1968 when six enthusiasts' specials toured the north-west to mark the end of regular steam on BR, one of them, the GC Enterprises tour to Carnforth, started and ended its journey at Stockport.

This volume in the 'Last Days of Steam Series' concentrates on the years 1964 to 1968, a time when steam aficionados increasingly made their way to such places as Birkenhead, Chester, Crewe, Northwich and Stockport to witness some of the dying embers of steam on BR. In those heady days I made numerous forays from my Lancashire home to the other side of the Mersey, either by train or bike, in order to imbibe steam and the following pages provide but a brief overview of the prevailing atmosphere of those times. For those who were there on the ground, they will never be forgotten.

While the curtain was brought down on steam by BR in August 1968, due to the vision and endeavour of the preservation movement, steam has continued to gladden the hearts of many people from time to time by its use on special services. This was the scene at Chester on 30 June 1991 when Stanier Pacific No. 46229 *Duchess of Hamilton* passed through en route from Holyhead to Crewe with a return 'North Wales Coast Express'.

The modernisation of the railways meant that evocative scenes such as this at the east end of Chester station, where 'Jubilee' class 4-6-0 No. 45647 *Sturdee* has paused with the 13.15 Llandudno to Manchester Exchange service on 22 August 1966, would soon be confined to history. With the driver looking on, the fireman takes the opportunity to drop the 'bag' into the tender in order to top up the contents while four teenagers observe matters from the leading carriage windows. Note, too, the lower quadrant signals, the brazier at the foot of the water column, and the wooden 'sentry box' available as shelter for crews waiting to relieve enginemen on incoming trains. During the 1960s the vast numbers of steam locomotives being made redundant meant BR no longer had the capacity to deal with the breaking of these at their own works and thousands were sold to privately owned scrapyards, *Sturdee* being towed to J. Cashmore's yard at Great Bridge, near Tipton, Staffordshire, after withdrawal in April 1967. Over one hundred yards participated in this macabre exercise. Similarly, much of the surrounding infrastructure from the steam age was also swept away in the ensuing years.

Facing page: During the 1960s when BR was disposing of its stock of steam locomotives, likewise so too those that had charge of operations along various dock lines, factories and other industrial locations across Cheshire, were also rapidly being phased out of existence. A reminder of those former days took place on Saturday 22 July 1978 when Liverpool Locomotive Preservation Group-owned 0-6-0ST *Lucy*, built by the Bristol-based Avonside Engine Company in 1909, works No. 1568, toured the Mersey Docks & Harbour Board's extensive rail system at Birkenhead. Passengers were accommodated in four brake vans and three mineral wagons, all suitably cleaned for the occasion. Here *Lucy* hauls its unusual load between the mobile cranes alongside East Float. Creeping along behind is 0-4-0 diesel-mechanical loco *Pegasus*, a product of Vulcan Foundry in 1949 and owned since 1962 by master porters and stevedores Rea Bulk Handling Ltd for use at the docks. Prior to preservation in 1972 *Lucy* was owned by Hutchinson Estate & Dock Co. (Widnes) Ltd at Widnes Harbour on the Lancashire side of the Mersey. At the time of this photograph *Lucy* was housed at Steamport Transport Museum, Southport, but following its closure in 1997 she has resided at the Ribble Steam Railway in Preston.

The stark reality of steam for those at the sharp end as a couple of enginemen at Stockport Edgeley shed shovel coal onto the elevator while loading the tender of 'Britannia' class Pacific No. 70013 *Oliver Cromwell* on 13 April 1968. The enormity of the task can be appreciated from the fact such tenders could hold up to seven tons of coal.

Facing page: In this view at Northwich shed on 25 February 1968 the foreground is littered with unsightly heaps of ash and clinker, laboriously raked out from the smokeboxes and ashpans of locomotives that had returned to the shed. A seemingly never ending task, this was never a pleasant job at the best of times, but even less so when strong winds were gusting around the site. Resting close up to another member of the class is Stanier 8F 2-8-0 No. 48036, which had been transferred to Northwich from Crewe South the previous March. Constructed at Vulcan Foundry, Newton-le-Willows, Lancashire, in 1936, life for No. 48036 was fast ebbing away, the locomotive being condemned the following week.

On this and the opposite page are representatives of the three main classes of locomotives that held sway across Cheshire during the last few years of steam. No. 92026 seen inside Birkenhead shed on 28 June 1966 was one of 251 BR Standard 9F 2-10-0s built between 1954 and 1960, 198 at Crewe and the remainder at Swindon, for heavy freight duties. However while Nos. 92045–47 were allocated to Bidston shed from the mid-1950s, specifically to handle the iron ore traffic from Birkenhead Docks for John Summers steelworks at Shotton, it was not until 1963 that the class became common across the rest of county, after being displaced elsewhere by the ongoing rush to dieselise services as quickly as possible. The sheer bulk of the 9Fs is apparent in this picture, No. 92026 being one of ten initially fitted at Crewe in 1955 with a Crosti boiler. All ten were allocated to Wellingborough, but the expected fuel savings by use of the pre-heater installed below the main boiler did not materialise and this, coupled with higher maintenance costs, led to the abandonment of the experiment in 1959. This example was the first to have the pre-heater removed, but with the smaller boilers retained and no smoke deflectors as per the rest of the class, the ex-Crostis were readily identifiable at a distance. On leaving Wellingborough in August 1963, No. 92026 subsequently served Kettering, Kirkby-in-Ashfield and Newton Heath sheds before moving to Birkenhead in May 1965.

Two of Sir William A. Stanier's masterpieces, Class 5 4-6-0 No. 44855 and 8F 2-8-0 No. 48549, in residence at Stockport Edgeley shed on 30 March 1968. No less than 842 Class 5s were put into service from 1934, the last not until 1951, and they quickly proved suitable for all manner of work. At Vesting Day, 1 January 1948, the LMS handed-over 742 of the class to the newly-formed British Railways, 195 built at Crewe, fifty-four at Derby and sixty-six at Horwich. Armstrong Whitworth of Newcastle-upon-Tyne and Vulcan Foundry of Newton-le-Willows, Lancashire, supplied 327 and 100 respectively during the 1930s and Crewe and Horwich constructed a further fifty each following Nationalisation, many with various modifications such as Caprotti valve gear and Timken or Skefko roller bearings. No. 44855 left Crewe Works new in 1944. The history of the 8Fs is even more complex. The prototype was outshopped from Crewe in 1935 and by 1939 the LMS had 126 on its books, fifty-seven manufactured at Crewe and sixty-nine built under contract by Vulcan Foundry. However the onset of the Second World War in 1939 meant there was an urgent need for more heavy freight engines for both home and overseas use and the Ministry of Supply decided the already proven 8F design would initially meet requirements. The necessary drawings were thus forwarded to the Southern Railway's Ashford, Brighton and Eastleigh works, the LNER shops at Darlington and Doncaster, the GWR Swindon Works and the LMS plant at Horwich. Others were put together by Beyer Peacock of Manchester and the North British Locomotive Company of Glasgow. In total 852 8Fs were built, the last in 1946. Many of those despatched overseas were destined never to return, eventually 666 being owned by BR, the last three being purchased from the Ministry of Defence as late as 1957. No. 48549 was a product of Darlington Works in 1945.

When the large sixteen-road depot at Birkenhead was commissioned in 1879 it was in essence two separate sheds, the Great Western and London & North Western railways each owning half the premises, with a wall defining the respective sections. In September 1950 forty-one engines that owed their allegiance to Swindon resided at the shed, ranging in size from a diminutive 1400 class 0-4-2T to a solitary 4700 class 2-8-0, six 'Grange' class 4-6-0s being the only named variety, while the other side of the divide was home to fifty locos of nine different classes previously owned by the LMS. Two ex-WD 2-8-0s were also on the books of the shed. However, by the 1960s all engines of a copper-capped variety had either been withdrawn or transferred elsewhere. The depot was first coded 6C by the LMS in 1935, this being retained by BR until 1963 when it was amended to 8H. It was also in 1963 that members of the BR Standard Class 9F 2-10-0s began to arrive at the shed, ten being transferred in that year, including six from nearby Bidston when that shed closed. Two years later the 9F allocation had multiplied to over fifty, and remarkably no less than sixty-seven of the class spent some time at Birkenhead. Here Nos. 92160 and 92089, along with Stanier 8F 2-8-0 No. 48676 visiting from Aintree, are pictured in the former GWR sector of the yard on 28 June 1966. The ferro-concrete coaling tower and the two ash disposal plants were erected by BR during the mid-1950s.

Two BR 9F 2-10-0s peep out from the shed at Birkenhead on 18 February 1966. Both were constructed at Crewe Works, No. 92107 in September 1956 and No. 92166 in May 1958, the latter one of three originally adapted with a Berkley mechanical stoker, although this fitment was removed four years later. During its relatively short career, previous to being one of the early 9F incomers to Birkenhead in February 1963, No. 92166 had worked from Saltley, Cardiff Canton, Newport Ebbw Junction and Bidston sheds. In contrast No. 92107 had been based at Wellingborough, Saltley, Banbury and Willesden before its move to the Wirral in December 1964. Both engines survived into 1967, No. 92107 being marked for the cutter's torch in February, its younger companion the following November when the shed bolted its doors to steam.

Hughes/Fowler 'Crab' 2-6-0 No. 42765 shuffles about the yard at Birkenhead on 28 June 1966. Released from Crewe Works when new in August 1927, the engine was transferred to Birkenhead from Fleetwood, where it had spent the previous thirteen years, in May 1964. When withdrawn in December 1966 it was one of the fortunate ones in that it was bought by scrap merchants Woodham Brothers of Barry, South Wales, where it lay derelict for over ten years before being purchased for preservation. Today the locomotive is a valued asset on the East Lancashire Railway at Bury.

BR Standard 9F 2-10-0 No. 92157 at Birkenhead shed, one of twenty-eight 9Fs logged by the author during a visit on the morning of 18 February 1966. The engine first saw the light of day at Crewe Works in November 1957, and was previously on the books of Toton and Saltley sheds before migrating north to Birkenhead in April 1964; it was withdrawn eighteen months later in August 1967. Slumbering in front of the 9F is ex-WD 2-8-0 No. 90351 which had clanked its way across the Pennines from its Mirfield home. During the years 1943 to 1945 the Ministry of Supply ordered 935 of these austere looking machines, 545 from the North British Locomotive Company of Glasgow, with the remainder supplied by Vulcan Foundry of Newton-le-Willows, Lancashire. The locomotives raison d'être was principally to assist the war effort overseas and once hostilities had ceased the majority were returned to Britain, 200 being bought by the LNER in December 1946, with a further 533 being added to BR stock following nationalisation. No. 90351 was a North British example from 1944, WD No. 77280; it was shipped to France in January 1945, returning home in September 1947, and after a period in storage was based at a number of sheds in the West Riding from 1950. It was condemned in September 1967. While certainly not the prettiest of locomotives on BR and slightly less powerful than the 9Fs, having a nominal tractive effort of 34,215lb against the 39,670lb of the latter, the WDs were very useful for heavy haulage duties and easy to maintain. Also recorded on the shed that day were two 2-6-4Ts (one to Stanier's specifications, the other a Fairburn development), two Hughes/Fowler 'Crab' 2-6-0s, two Fowler 'Jinty' 0-6-0Ts and four Stanier 8F 2-8-0s. Completing the tally but perhaps looking a little out of place was a solitary member of the new order, diesel shunter No. D2507.

Twenty years after the last of the withdrawn engines had been towed away from Birkenhead shed, steam made a welcome return to the Wirral during the Bank Holiday weekend of 30 April to 2 May 1988. The occasion was part of the celebrations to mark the centenary of Lever Brothers, when a shuttle service was provided along their internal railway from a temporary platform at Port Sunlight station to the Stork Margarine Works at Bromborough, a round trip of five miles that was last used by steam in the 1950s. Seen here in an industrial setting ex-GWR Churchward 2-6-2T No. 4566 from the Severn Valley Railway, with five coaches filled to capacity trailing behind, evoked many happy memories from the past on the opening day of the event.

Former LMS Fowler 'Jinty' 0-6-0T No. 7298, transported from the Llangollen Railway, was attached to the other end of the Bank Holiday train. Coincidentally both engines were built in 1924 and after withdrawal by BR, No. 4566 in April 1962 and No. 7298 in December 1966, they were purchased by Woodham Brothers of Barry. After slowly rotting for some years in the salty sea air at this South Wales scrapyard they were exhumed by preservationists, the former in August 1970 and the 'Jinty' in July 1974.

15

Facing page: In its heyday Hooton station, located half-a-mile west of the quiet village it served, had seven platforms. A three-way junction just south of the station enabled trains to branch off the main line to Chester to either Helsby or West Kirby. Prior to Nationalisation all three routes were jointly owned by the GWR and LMS. Running into platform 4 on 22 August 1966 with the 11.45 Birkenhead Woodside to London Paddington service, with Hooton North signal box protruding above the rear coaches, is Stanier 2-6-4T No. 42647, built at Derby Works in 1938. The locomotive was a newcomer to Birkenhead shed, having only arrived there the previous month from Springs Branch (Wigan).

Photographed a couple of minutes later on the same day, No. 42647 continues on its way to Chester, where it would be relieved by another locomotive for the onward journey towards the capital. Note the miniature signal arms on the gantry, the one formerly attached to the right-hand post having been removed when the line to West Kirby, which veered off to the right, was closed to goods traffic on 7 May 1962, passenger services having ceased on 17 September 1956. The layout was controlled from Hooton South signal box, seen behind the supporting gantry post. No. 42647 remained in service until May 1967.

The oil refineries at Stanlow, between Ellesmere Port and Helsby, provided plenty of revenue for BR, any trains destined for the Chester direction having to reverse at Hooton. All taken on 22 August 1966, the sequence of photographs on these two pages depicts the procedure. First BR Standard 9F 2-10-0 No. 92137 is seen (left) approaching the station tender-first from Stanlow, towing eleven loaded oil tanks of various designs and a couple of brake-vans. The line on the left led to a south facing bay platform. After the convoy had been parked in platform 3, the 2-10-0 was detached from the train, ran towards North signal box, crossed from the down to the up slow line and returned light engine through the station (lower left). Ten minutes later, having been re-coupled to its train, No. 92137 and with steam to spare (right) resumed its journey. This Crewe-built loco, after spending the first nine years of its life at Saltley, had been transferred to Croes Newydd shed (Wrexham) earlier that month. However its stay at Wrexham was brief, as it was relocated to Carlisle Kingmoor at the end of the year, where it survived until September 1967.

Seen here on 22 August 1966 as it rumbles into platform 2, a west facing bay at Chester General, with an afternoon Birkenhead to Paddington service, is Warrington-based Stanier 'Black 5' 4-6-0 No. 45312. The engine was still looking reasonably smart after a recent visit to Crewe Works for some light casual repairs. It was built for the LMS at Armstrong Whitworth's Newcastle-upon-Tyne factory in February 1937, remaining in traffic until June 1968 when it was designated for scrap at Bolton shed. The bunker of Stanier 2-6-4T No. 42616 from Birkenhead shed, which was biding time waiting to take over the next northbound service from Paddington, is prominent on the left. It was delivered to the LMS during the same month as the 'Black 5', but from the Glasgow-based North British Locomotive Company.

Seen on the same day, a few minutes after the scene captured opposite, the slightly older 'Black 5' No. 45231 (Armstrong Whitworth-built August 1936) is ready to leave the cathedral city with the Paddington bound carriages. No. 45231 would give way to a diesel locomotive at Shrewsbury for the rest of the journey south, extra coaches including a restaurant car being added at Wolverhampton. The engine was allocated to Chester shed from June 1963 until March 1967, whereupon after just over a year on the books of Speke Junction shed (Liverpool), it was maintained at Carnforth until the very end of BR steam in August 1968. A short while later it was purchased privately for preservation and can still be seen from time to time on the main lines at the head of steam excursions. No. 42616 on the right was not quite so fortunate, being sold for scrap after its withdrawal in September 1967. Nosing into the frame on the left is Stanier 8F 2-8-0 No. 48527 from Stoke shed.

Another of the Armstrong Whitworth batch of Stanier Class 5 4-6-0s, No. 45238, treads the up centre through road at Chester with a lengthy train of vans of various descriptions from Holyhead on 22 August 1966. The station ironwork is worthy of study, although the near footbridge has since been dismantled. During its career, which started at Chester in August 1936, No. 45238 was reallocated between sheds on no less than eighteen occasions, finally ending its days at Warrington from September 1964, where it was retired in December 1966.

The efficient operation of many large stations often depended on the station pilot, as at Chester where Fowler 'Jinty' 0-6-0T No. 47507, here running into an east end bay, had been assigned this duty on 22 August 1966. Note the large running-in board on the left clearly stating this to be Chester General, while the lamps of more recent vintage are inscribed plain Chester, this despite the ex-CLC Chester Northgate station still being in existence and remaining so until 6 October 1969. No. 47507, constructed by Vulcan Foundry in April 1928, was in fact at the disposal of the Chester shed foreman for only a matter of weeks after its move from Llandudno Junction in mid-July, for within three weeks of this picture being recorded it was laid aside for scrap.

A prominent feature at the east end of Chester station was the array of former LNWR lower quadrant signals operated from Chester No. 2 signal box, to be seen in the right background in this view from Bank Holiday Monday 3 August 1964. Stanier Class 5 4-6-0 No. 44766, the next-to-last example constructed by the LMS at Crewe in December 1947, and experimentally fitted with Timken roller bearings and a double chimney, has permission to depart, while June 1950 Horwich-built No. 44682 with Skefko roller bearings backs down towards the platforms. The former was based at Bescot shed (Walsall), but spent the period from October 1966 to April 1967 at Chester shed before a final move to Crewe South. No. 44682 was then midway through a three month sojourn at Chester, prior to a transfer to Stoke before ending its days at Springs Branch (Wigan) from August 1967. Both locomotives were withdrawn during 1967, No. 44766 in August and No. 44682 in December.

On the same sunny afternoon unkempt Aston-allocated 'Britannia' class 4-6-2 No. 70016 *Ariel* departs Chester while returning to the Midlands from a trip along the North Wales coast. The Pacific first took to the rails at Crewe Works in June 1951 and during its comparatively short life was based at eleven sheds ranging from Stratford (London) and Laira (Plymouth) in the south, to Carlisle in the north where it was finally deemed unserviceable at Kingmoor in August 1967.

By 1964 the English Electric Type 4 2,000hp diesel-electric locomotives (later Class 40) were quite common at Chester, where No. D269 on the same day as the previous two pictures, awaits the signal to depart with another Bank Holiday service from North Wales. Seemingly standing defiant behind with its safety valves emitting excess steam, is locally-based 1935 Armstrong Whitworth-built Class 5 4-6-0 No. 45130, a Chester engine from June 1963 until September 1965. It became available to the scrap metal industry when Birkenhead shed closed in November 1967. No. D269 had a shorter lifespan, leaving Vulcan Foundry in April 1960 it was withdrawn in September 1983.

The former LNWR motive power depot at Chester, located east of the station within the 'V' of the lines to Crewe and Warrington, dated from 1870. In 1935 the shed was coded 6A by the LMS, which it retained throughout its existence. In 1950 under BR the shed had responsibility for thirty-eight ex-LMS locos, the total having risen to forty-six, including twenty-five built to BR Standard designs by 1959. The next year it became the sole steam depot in the city when the ex-GWR and the old CLC Northgate sheds both barred their doors to the iron horse. At the start of 1967 the allocation had reduced to thirty, composed of twenty-three Stanier Class 5 4-6-0s, five Stanier 8F 2-8-0s and a couple of BR Standard Class 4 2-6-0s. The shed closed a few months later on 5 June 1967. The previous year, on the gloomy afternoon (weather wise!) of 18 February 1966, following the instructions in the indispensable *British Locomotive Shed Directory*, the author undertook the twenty-five-minute walk from the station to Hoole Lane, from where a cinder path led to the shed. Noted 'on shed' during the visit were ten Stanier Class 5 4-6-0s, a 'Jubilee' class 4-6-0 (see next page), two 'Jinty' 0-6-0Ts Nos. 47324 and 47389, 8F 2-8-0 No. 48287 and four BR Standards Nos. 75010, 76085, 76095 and 92086. Two diesel shunters were also present. The photographs on these and the following two pages were taken that day.

Facing page: Stanier Class 5 4-6-0 No. 45031, built by Vulcan Foundry in 1934, has just arrived back at its home base, where it had resided since June 1963, access to the shed being gained from the Crewe line, in the shadow of the gable ends of the terraced rows on the left. Coaling here, by means of the elevator, was a somewhat rudimentary affair. The raised semaphore signal behind the elevator is by the Warrington line.

Right: Resting inside the eight-road shed, flanked by a couple of Stanier Class 5 4-6-0s, is BR Standard Class 4 2-6-0 No. 76085 from Stoke shed, not Saltley as stencilled beneath the grime on the buffer beam which referred to a previous posting. The 2-6-0 was undergoing some remedial work with parts of its motion seemingly strewn haphazardly on the ground. The open pits and the old planking also vividly portray the day to day hazards of working in such places, although up the near the roof between the smoke hoods the lighting provision appears reasonably adequate. No. 76085 was a Horwich-built engine from 1957, but by this time it had not long for this world, being withdrawn the following July from Colwick shed, near Nottingham.

Visiting Chester from Farnley Junction shed (Leeds) is Stanier three-cylinder 'Jubilee' class 4-6-0 No. 45647 *Sturdee*. The nameplate was a wooden replica, the original having been removed a couple of years earlier, while the diagonal yellow stripe across the cab side-sheet indicated it was not to work south of Crewe under the electrified wires due to clearance constraints. In total 191 'Jubilees' were built between 1934 and 1936, *Sturdee* emerging from Crewe Works in January 1935, but by 1966 only fifteen remained in traffic, eight surviving into 1967. These included *Sturdee* and by that time it had clocked over 1,400,000 miles.

The fireman leaning out of the cab on Stoke-allocated (5D) Stanier 8F 2-8-0 No. 48018 surveys the shed yard at Chester, while passing on the line towards Crewe with a rake of mineral wagons in tow. The locomotive had an interesting history. Constructed by the LMS at Crewe Works in 1937, it was requisitioned by the Ministry of Supply in 1941, converted to oil firing, fitted with a cowcatcher and air brakes, and despatched to Iran at the end of the year. As WD No. 70582 it was repatriated during April 1948, subsequently starting its BR days in December 1949. The loco was based at Stoke from January 1965 until March 1967, after earlier working from Crewe South, Warwick, Northampton and Rugby sheds. It spent its final few months on the books of Crewe South and Chester sheds, before being withdrawn in October 1967.

From a small two-platform station established by the Grand Junction Railway in 1837, Crewe grew into one of the most important railway centres in Britain. The catalyst for much of the town's growth was the decision by the Grand Junction to move its workshop facilities from Edge Hill (Liverpool) to Crewe - the new works opening on a small three-acre site in 1843. In 1846 the Grand Junction became part of the newly-formed London & North Western Railway and under their direction the works gradually expanded over 137 acres. At its peak the factory employed over 8,500 men. During the last months of steam activity at Crewe, Stanier Class 5 4-6-0 No. 44678 drags some parcels vans from the sidings south of the station on 27 May 1967. The engine departed Horwich Works new in May 1950, the first of eight 'Black 5s' experimentally equipped with Skefko roller bearings to all axles. The engine was shedded successively at Crewe North, Holyhead, Carlisle Upperby, Crewe North again, Rugby, Crewe North for a third time, Crewe South and Speke Junction (Liverpool), before its final move to Springs Branch (Wigan) in January 1966. There its days ended in November 1967.

A little later No. 44678 departs north across Crewe North Junction, the three leading parcels vans each being to a different design. The tracks veering to the left beneath the locomotive led to Chester, while those branching off to the right are followed by trains bound for Manchester. The flat-roofed Crewe North signal box can just be discerned above No. 44678, this now being part of Crewe Heritage Centre (see page 33). The BR steam era at Crewe concluded with the closure of South shed (code 5B) on 6 November 1967, steam having been dispensed with at North shed (5A) on 24 May 1965. Only a few years earlier in 1959 over 240 steam locomotives had been allocated between the two sheds.

It could be argued the steam age has never actually ended at Crewe, with many steam specials having graced its platforms in more recent times. Here the unique BR Standard Class 8P 4-6-2 No. 71000 *Duke of Gloucester*, fitted with Caprotti valve gear, propels two coaches towards the platforms for attaching to a much longer rake to form a 'North Wales Coast Express' to Holyhead on Sunday 5 August 1990. Note the expectant passengers lining the platform. The Pacific perhaps looks a little incongruous surrounded by metalwork and electrified overhead wiring, while three representatives of its motive power successors are also in sight. Appropriately a 5A (Crewe North) shedplate has been attached to the smokebox door; it was on the books of the depot after emerging from the nearby works in May 1954 (apart from a few months at Swindon under test) until its deletion from capital stock in November 1962. It was then stored for nearly five years before being towed to Woodham Brothers scrapyard at Barry, South Wales, in October 1967, but only after the left-hand cylinder and valve gear had been removed for display in the Science Museum in London. 'The Duke' was rescued from potential oblivion in April 1974, and its subsequent return to the main line is one of the most notable achievements of the steam preservation movement.

From relatively humble beginnings in 1843 Crewe Works completed no less than 7,331 steam locomotives, the last being BR 9F 2-10-0 No. 92250 in December 1958. Following Privatisation in 1989 the works has continued to serve the rail industry, although on a much reduced scale compared to former LNWR, LMS and BR days. In more recent times, a number of what proved very popular Open Days have been organised at the works and seen here on the eve of one on Friday 16 August 1996, Stanier 'Princess Coronation' Class 8P 4-6-2 No. 46229 *Duchess of Hamilton*, back at its birthplace where it was built by the LMS in September 1938, slowly edges its way onto the traverser. The engine originally sported a streamlined profile for hauling Anglo-Scottish expresses; it gained a more conventional look in November 1947 when the streamlined casing was removed. After withdrawal in February 1964 it was bought for display at Butlin's Minehead Holiday Camp in Somerset; it was retrieved from there in March 1975 and transported to the embryonic National Railway Museum at York. The Pacific was returned to running order in 1980 but has since reverted to its early LMS streamlined guise as a static exhibit at York. Mention should also be made of Crewe Heritage Centre, established adjacent to the West Coast main line on part of the works site in 1987, where steam locomotives and more modern forms of traction can be enjoyed.

Stanier 'Black 5' 4-6-0 No. 45135 hurries along the West Coast main line towards Crewe at Preston Brook with a lengthy freight on 8 July 1967. In the distance, beyond Norton Crossing signal box, is the six-arch viaduct that supports the Chester–Warrington line. No. 45135 was constructed by Armstrong Whitworth in May 1935, one of a batch of 100 manufactured by the company that year. Since November 1964 it had been shedded at Carlisle Kingmoor and by this time, although daily mileage details had ceased to be maintained, it is highly likely to have completed over one million miles, as by 1960 it had travelled over 936,000 miles. However its time as a useful asset was fast running out, as it was taken out of service the following October.

Following closely behind No. 45135 southbound on the same day at Preston Brook, Kingmoor colleague 'Britannia' Pacific No. 70011 *Hotspur* (the nameplates having been removed) has charge of a rake of empty mineral wagons. This was somewhat of a comedown for *Hotspur* compared to the first ten years of its existence when based at Norwich from May 1951, where it was regularly diagrammed to crack East Anglian expresses between there and London Liverpool Street. It was displaced from Norwich in September 1961 and found a new home at March shed, but then in December 1963 it headed north to Carlisle after transfer from Eastern to London Midland Region stock. Its last years were spent at the Border City attached at times to both Upperby and Kingmoor sheds, prior to its withdrawal from the latter in December 1967. There is now no trace of the former station at Preston Brook, situated just beyond the overbridge, which closed on 1 March 1948. The picture was captured from the aqueduct that enables barges on the Runcorn branch of the Bridgewater Canal to float over the railway.

A set of water troughs were provided at Moore, two miles north of Preston Brook, where locomotives could replenish their water supplies while on the move, thus saving time at stations or having to stop specifically for the purpose. Here BR Standard 9F 2-10-0 No. 92125 trundles south over the troughs on 1 July 1967. The tall building just beyond the back of the train was the water softening plant. Passenger trains ceased to call at Moore station, situated in the cutting behind the brake van, from 1 February 1943. No. 92125 left Crewe Works new in March 1957, initially working from Wellingborough shed before moving to Kettering (December 1960), Saltley (November 1963), Croes Newydd (May 1966) and Carlisle Kingmoor in December 1966. It was condemned at the latter in December 1967 and its 101-ton bulk was subsequently dismembered by Arnott Young at their Parkgate & Rawmarsh yard, near Rotherham.

During the same afternoon a second Carlisle Kingmoor-allocated locomotive, 'Britannia' class 4-6-2 No. 70035 *Rudyard Kipling*, was observed scurrying over the troughs with a northbound parcels train. This December 1952 Crewe-built Pacific was on the books of Norwich shed until May 1958 when it was moved to March. It returned to Norwich the following January, but left East Anglia permanently in October 1961 when assigned to Immingham shed. A move back to March in June 1963 preceded a final transfer at the end of that year to Kingmoor, where it continued to earn its keep for another four years. In March 1968 it was towed to T.W. Ward's Inverkeithing yard in Fife for disposal.

Freshly reallocated to Northwich shed from Aintree only the previous month, Stanier 8F 2-8-0 No. 48340 coasts down the 1-in-135 gradient from Acton Grange Junction, as it heads for home with a freight consisting mainly of chemical tanks on 1 July 1967. The flat-topped forty-lever signal box that controlled the junction can be discerned behind the brake van. The train had entered Cheshire a minute or so earlier after crossing the Mersey soon after leaving Warrington; the girder bridge in the background, a little south of the river, spans the January 1894-opened Manchester Ship Canal. Before the canal could be completed it was necessary to construct over a mile of steeply-inclined railway either side of the new waterway, so as to create sufficient headroom beneath the bridge to allow ocean going vessels to sail inland to Cottonopolis. In view on the right, climbing towards the junction with the West Coast main line is the Chester–Warrington line, while nearer the camera at a lower level is the trackbed of the original line from Crewe. Note the in-filled overbridge on the old formation, to be seen above the locomotive cab. When Northwich shed bade farewell to steam at the beginning of March 1968, this Horwich 1944-built 8F transferred its affections to Rose Grove (Burnley), but only for one month, before a three-month spell at Bolton preceded a return to Rose Grove, where it remained active until the beginning of August 1968.

Photographed on the same day, BR Standard 9F 2-10-0s Nos. 92054 (of Speke Junction shed, Liverpool) and 92082 (Birkenhead) drift downhill from Acton Grange Junction along the line towards Chester, while en route to Birkenhead shed. Note the cutting on the right-hand side of the picture which was threaded by the Chester line before the coming of the Manchester Ship Canal necessitated its realignment. Also note the catch-points by the 9Fs to prevent runaways from trains climbing the bank escaping too far. Both locomotives were products of Crewe Works, No. 92054 in September 1955 and No. 92082 in May 1956, but within one year both had been deemed surplus to requirements, the latter in November 1967 when Birkenhead shed closed to steam, while the former soldiered on until the following May when Speke Junction ceased to service steam.

Stanier 8F 2-8-0 No. 48727 is about to pass over the barrow crossing at the west end of Helsby station with a train of vans travelling towards Warrington from Chester on 11 August 1967. The sign on the right headed L&NW & GW Joint Lines, stating that only the companies servants must use the crossing, betrays the antecedence of the route, in that prior to the Grouping in 1923 it was jointly owned by the two companies and usually referred to as the Birkenhead Joint. The bridge in the background carries ex-Cheshire Lines Committee tracks whereby trains from the Hooton direction could reach Mouldsworth and gain access to the Chester-Manchester via Northwich route. Sanctioned by the Ministry of Supply, No. 48727 was among a batch of twenty-five new 8Fs constructed by the Southern Railway's Brighton Works in 1944 for the LNER. They were passed to the LMS in 1946/47. Since the previous May No. 48727 had been on the books of Northwich shed after transfer from Sutton Oak (St Helens); it survived in BR service until August 1968.

Nearing the end of its comparatively short existence of less than ten years, BR Standard 9F 2-10-0 No. 92234 clatters through Helsby in the opposite direction with some westbound empty cattle vans on the same day as the picture opposite. Worthy of note are the architectural details of the station building, the enclosed footbridge and staircases, and the 45-lever signal box dating from 1900. Platforms 3 and 4 serving the line from Hooton via Ellesmere Port are out of sight to the left; the connections with the Chester lines can be discerned just beyond the footbridge. The co-acting signal, partially visible behind the near lamppost, was to aid drivers of Warrington-bound trains from the Chester direction. New from Crewe Works in August 1958, No. 92234 had periods of duty at Pontypool Road, Severn Tunnel Junction, Cardiff Canton, Banbury (three separate postings), Bromsgrove, Tyseley and Saltley sheds, before moving to Birkenhead in December 1966. It was deleted from the BR stock list in November 1967.

The front end of BR Standard 9F 2-10-0 No. 92054, visiting from Speke Junction shed, dominates this view of Northwich shed yard, taken on Sunday 25 February 1968. To be seen scattered around the yard are ten Stanier 8F 2-8-0s plus three Sulzer Type 2 (later Class 25) diesel locomotives. Following Nationalisation in January 1948 this former Cheshire Lines Committee depot (the building is out of sight to the right of the picture) was initially placed under control of the Eastern Region but by the end of the year had become part of the London Midland Region, even though at the time its allocation consisted entirely of locomotives with a Great Central Railway pedigree. This was soon to change as more and more ex-LMS engines were drafted in, but it was not until February 1960 that the last of the former GCR locos, Class J10 0-6-0 No. 65169, by then over sixty years old, was disposed of. When BR decided to adopt the former LMS depot coding system, the shed was first identified in 1949 as 13D, but the plates hardly had time to be fitted before it was changed to 9G. In 1958 the code was amended to 8E.

At the start of 1968 Northwich shed had responsibility for seventeen steam locomotives (a reduction from forty-two in 1950), all Stanier 8F 2-8-0s. Here on the same day as the photograph opposite two of the home-based fleet, work-stained Nos. 48632 and 48272, face each other across the 70ft-diameter turntable. The latter was built by the North British Locomotive Company, Glasgow, in June 1942, while No. 48632 was completed at the Southern Railway Brighton Works in June of the following year. The pair were both retired a week later.

Again on Sunday 25 February 1968 four more Stanier 8F 2-8-0s stand ready for what would be the final week of steam activity at Northwich shed. The goings-on at the shed could readily be observed from the adjacent station platforms, as visible on the right-hand side of the frame. The depot officially closed to steam from Monday 4 March 1968.

After March 1968 the shed continued as a stabling point for diesel locomotives, but occasionally in the early 1980s steam made a welcome return. Here on Saturday 20 June 1981, far from its old haunts on former Southern Railway territory, preserved Maunsell 'Lord Nelson' class 4-6-0 No. 850 *Lord Nelson*, built at Eastleigh in 1926, poses outside the four-road brick-built shed. At the time *Lord Nelson* was normally housed at Steamtown Railway Museum, Carnforth, and was at Northwich prior to hauling a special to Leeds. The site was finally abandoned by BR in November 1984, the area now being covered by a private housing estate.

A vivid reminder of times past at Northwich on 1 February 1992 when preserved Stanier 8F 2-8-0 No. 48773 headed a special through the town, and is seen approaching the station from the Chester direction. The engine was making its way from the Severn Valley Railway to visit the Keighley & Worth Valley Railway. The engine has had a charmed existence to say the least. It started life in June 1940 when released from the North British Locomotive Company Hyde Park Works in Glasgow as WD No. 307, part of an order for the Ministry of Supply intended for war service in France. In the event, following a change of plan, it was first loaned to the LMS before being reclaimed by the WD in September 1941 and shipped to Iran, fortunately surviving the journey, unlike some of its classmates that were lost at sea. In 1946 it was loaned to the Egyptian State Railways where it almost met its demise two years later when stopped with a badly damaged firebox. However in 1950 it was decided to repatriate the engine and after an overhaul at Derby Works moved to the Longmoor Military Railway in Hampshire. It was purchased by BR in 1957, along with two of its sisters, and given the number 48773. Allocated to Polmadie shed in Glasgow, it was withdrawn in December 1962, only to be restored to stock the next month. It was deleted from capital stock for a second time the following June, but reprieved yet again in November when it was transferred from Scottish to London Midland Region stock and attached successively to the sheds at Carlisle Kingmoor, Stockport Edgeley, Buxton, Bolton and lastly Rose Grove (Burnley), from where it was withdrawn (for a third time!) on 4 August 1968. The next month, after purchase by the Stanier 8F Locomotive Society, it was moved to secure accommodation on the infant Severn Valley Railway at Bridgnorth, Shropshire, where it continues to be well cared for.

Running tender-first, Stanier 8F 2-8-0 No. 48723 drifts by the lofty Skelton Junction signal box, while on its way back to Heaton Mersey shed on 27 April 1968. On former Cheshire Lines Committee territory, the tracks leading straight ahead beyond the signal box continued to Glazebrook where they joined the old CLC Manchester-Warrington-Liverpool route, while those veering to the left led to the former London & North Western line to Warrington Arpley. The rails to be seen above the 8F (the only ones still open) swing round through ninety degrees to pass beneath the long footbridge and the other two routes to reach Altrincham and Northwich. No. 48723 was among the same batch of 8Fs as No. 48727 built for the London & North Eastern Railway at Brighton Works in 1944 (see page 40). After hostilities had ceased it too was transferred to the LMS. When Heaton Mersey shed closed a week later it was moved to Lostock Hall shed (Preston), where it lasted until the beginning of August 1968.

Facing page: Travelling in the opposite direction at Skelton Junction on the same day with a train of loose-coupled loaded mineral wagons, is Edge Hill (Liverpool)-allocated Stanier Class 5 4-6-0 No. 45282. The raised semaphore indicates it is about to follow the route towards Warrington Arpley. The locomotive was one of 327 'Black 5s' constructed by Armstrong Whitworth for the LMS between 1935 and 1937, this example leaving their Scotswood, Newcastle-upon-Tyne factory in November 1936. It remained active in the area during the following week but was then withdrawn.

Facing page: The former Cheshire Lines Committee shed at Heaton Mersey, one mile west of Stockport Tiviot Dale station, was actually on the north side of the River Mersey in Lancashire, but is included in this volume in that engines departing the depot, in either direction, were almost immediately back on Cheshire soil. Further, the only means of access on foot was from the Cheshire side of the Mersey by means of a narrow footbridge over the river. When the eight-road shed first opened in 1889 the facilities were shared by the Manchester, Sheffield & Lincolnshire (Great Central from 1897) and Midland railways, an arrangement continued by the LNER and LMS after the Grouping in 1923. During the early days of BR locomotives from both constituents remained on the allocation list; for instance in September 1950 the shed was home to twenty-eight former LNER and thirty-six ex-LMS locos. However, as the 1950s progressed the Eastern's influence steadily declined and the last remaining example, J10 0-6-0 No. 65194, was withdrawn at the end of 1959. By the start of 1967 the allocation consisted entirely of locomotives designed by Stanier, thirteen Class 5 4-6-0s and twenty-six 8F 2-8-0s, their ranks being reduced to six Class 5s and twenty 8Fs by January 1968. For the majority of its days under BR the shed was coded 9F. Here, 1942 North British-built 8F No. 48191, resident at Heaton Mersey since being moved from Wellingborough during the winter of 1957, simmers outside the shed on 4 May 1968. The star below the number indicates that 50% of its reciprocating weight had been balanced, which enabled it to be employed on faster freight services.

Right: A week earlier at Heaton Mersey on 27 April 1968, another 1942 North British-built 8F No. 48278 stands alongside the coaling stage. The contents of the wagons on the left were unloaded manually into wheeled tubs ready for tipping into locomotive tenders or bunkers; one of the hinged ramps used for this purpose can be seen protruding from the platform. In contrast to No. 48191 *(opposite)*, No. 48278 had only been available to the shed foreman at Heaton Mersey for some four months after its transfer from Patricroft at the beginning of the year. Presumably the depot had no cast 9F plates left, the code having been rather crudely painted on the smokebox door. When the shed closed the following weekend both engines depicted on these two pages left for Rose Grove shed (Burnley), where they eked out their last days until that shed closed at the beginning of August 1968.

On Saturday 4 May 1968, two days before the official closure of Heaton Mersey, Carnforth-allocated BR Standard 9F 2-10-0 No. 92118 along with Stanier 8F 2-8-0s Nos. 48319 and 48356 await the signal to leave the shed for the very last time. On the right is the soon to be defunct coaling stage, while by the main line on the left is one of the distinctive CLC water columns. Just to the left of the 9F's tender can be glimpsed a Brush Type 4 and a couple of Sulzer Type 2 diesel locomotives, symbolic of the power that within a matter of hours would have full command of the area. Both the 8Fs were completed by the LMS in 1944, No. 48319 at Crewe and No. 48356 at Horwich. The pair were comparative newcomers to Heaton Mersey, the former arriving from Patricroft at the turn of the year, No. 48356 coming from Trafford Park at the beginning of March.

After the trio had moved onto the main line by Heaton Mersey West signal box, an enthusiast reluctantly jumps down from the cab of No. 48319 as they set off in the direction of Stockport, the 8Fs to pastures new (No. 48319 to Bolton and No. 48356 to Newton Heath) and No. 92118 back to Carnforth. Poignantly reminiscent of such occasions are the epitaphs chalked on the tender of the leading locomotive 'Last Run Out RIP' and 'Last Day of Steam at 9F'. The girder bridge overhead carried the ex-Midland Railway direct route from Chinley to Manchester Central, while the bridge beyond at the lower level spans the Mersey, Cheadle Junction signal box in the background being in Cheshire. Within a month all three locomotives had been condemned.

Facing page: The eight-road Stockport Edgeley shed was opened by the London & North Western Railway in May 1883; throughout its eighty-five year existence its allocation was utilised mainly on non-passenger work. The code 9B was conferred on the depot by the LMS in 1935 and retained until its closure on 6 May 1968. It had twenty-seven engines on its books in September 1950, and perhaps surprisingly thirty-nine at the start of 1967, including four 'Britannia' Pacifics for parcels duties. Numbers had been reduced to twenty-two at the start of 1968, twelve 'Black 5' 4-6-0s and ten 8F 2-8-0s. A feature at many ex-LNWR sheds was a substantial brick-built coaling stage with a large water tank on top, the wagon road being steeply ramped to assist shovelling the heavy fuel into waiting tenders and bunkers. Even so much back-breaking work was involved, and this was only eased at Stockport in 1962 when an electrically-driven conveyor was obtained (see page 8). Posing outside the 'coal hole' on Saturday 27 April 1968 is a very smart looking Stanier 8F 2-8-0 No. 48652, complete with mini-snowplough but devoid of any shed identification plate. The engine had arrived a little earlier at Edgeley Junction from Bolton with the joint Manchester Rail Travel/Severn Valley Railway societies' 'North West Tour' (see inside front cover), which had started that morning from Birmingham New Street. Earlier in the day 'Black 5s' Nos. 44781 and 45046 had headed the special from Stockport via Buxton and Chinley to Stalybridge, where they had been relieved by BR Standard Class 5 4-6-0s Nos. 73050 and 73069 for the onward journey to Huddersfield, Burnley and Bolton. No. 48652 was a product of Eastleigh Works in November 1943, one of twenty-three put together at this Southern Railway plant. It was taken out of service two months later when the fires were dropped for the last time at Bolton shed.

Right: Alongside the 'coal hole' on the ash pit road at Stockport, the driver climbs down from a very grubby home-based 8F 2-8-0 No. 48745 on 30 March 1968. The coal conveyor can be seen behind the loco. No. 48745 was manufactured by the LNER at their Darlington factory in April 1946 and had been on the register at Stockport since October 1966 after transfer from Agecroft. It finally succumbed to the inevitable when the shed closed five weeks later.

A distinguished visitor to Stockport Edgeley shed on 13 April 1968 was the sole-surviving 'Britannia' class 4-6-2 No. 70013 *Oliver Cromwell*, based at Carnforth shed (10A) for special duties during the last months of BR steam. It had arrived from Hellifield where it had taken over a BR Scottish Region sponsored 'Easter Grand Tour' from Edinburgh. While the engine was serviced the excursion went on to Stafford and back behind an electric locomotive. Here *Oliver Cromwell* cautiously noses its way onto the turntable. The water tank above the 'coal hole' is conspicuous on the left, while on the right is the electrified main line linking Manchester Piccadilly with London Euston. Later the Pacific powered the returning special as far as Carnforth (see inside back cover).

A rather unkempt double-chimney BR Standard 9F 2-10-0 No. 92218 is swung round on the 60 foot-diameter, vacuum-operated turntable at Stockport Edgeley shed on 27 April 1968. Its 55ft 11in. wheelbase (including tender) necessitated careful positioning and the total length of 66ft 2in. over buffers meant there was some overhang at each end. The 9F had travelled from Speke Junction shed, where it was allocated, to take charge of the final steam leg of the 'North West Tour' (see pages 52-53) to Liverpool Lime Street. It would appear little attempt had been made at its Merseyside home to spruce up the loco for its roll in the limelight. On the left a Stanier 'Black 5' 4-6-0 stands outside the shed, while an English Electric Type 4 diesel infiltrates the scene on the right. No. 92218 was one of the last three steam locomotives built for BR at Swindon Works in 1960 (the last, No. 92220 *Evening Star*, left in March). It started its career on the Western Region at Bristol St Philips Marsh shed, moving to Old Oak Common (London) in September 1960 and then Banbury in March 1963, where it became London Midland Region property from September 1963 due to regional boundary changes. It was later reallocated by the LMR to Warrington, Speke Junction and Carlisle Kingmoor, before returning to Speke in January 1968.

No. 92218 pulls away from Edgeley Junction after taking charge of the 'North West Tour' for the onward journey to Liverpool via the ex-Cheshire Lines Committee route through Northenden and Warrington. Prior to departure there had been time to replace the number plate and hide some rather untidy painted numerals (see previous page), affix a MRTS board and the reporting number 1Z77 to the centre lamp bracket. Unnecessarily and doing nothing whatsoever to enhance its appearance, the latter had also been scrawled on the smokebox door. It could be described as scandalous that after a life of little more than eight years, the engine was condemned the next month, although it must be said many of its classmates enjoyed even shorter existences. Scrap dealers Arnott Young of Parkgate and Rawmarsh, near Rotherham, were responsible for its destruction during July 1968.